BOOK OF THE TAROT

AN INTRODUCTION TO THE TAROT CARDS

CALIBER
COMICS

BOOK OF THE TAROT

An Introduction to the Tarot Cards

Written and compiled by
GARY REED

Production by:
Nathan Pride
Gary Reed

CALIBER
COMICS

ILLUSTRATORS

The Fool	Chris Caldwell
The Magician	John Marroquin
The High Priestess	Mark Bloodworth
The Empress	Don England
The Emperor	Seth Damoose
The Hierophant	Vincent Locke
The Lovers	Ted Woods
The Chariot	Robert Knight
Strength	Derek Rook
The Hermit	Bruce Gerlach
Wheel of Fortune	Aimee Anderson
Justice	Tony Casteel
The Hanged Man	Joseph Cooper
Death	Bill Pulkovski
Temperance	Anna Garavaglia
The Devil	Jim Demick
The Tower	Tony Miello
The Star	Anjie Conway
The Moon	Nathan Pride
The Sun	MV Romanova
Judgment	Jason Westlake
The World	Kelly O'Hara
King of Wands	Terry Pavlet

Cover Image by: Cyril van der Haegen

BOOK
OF THE
TAROT

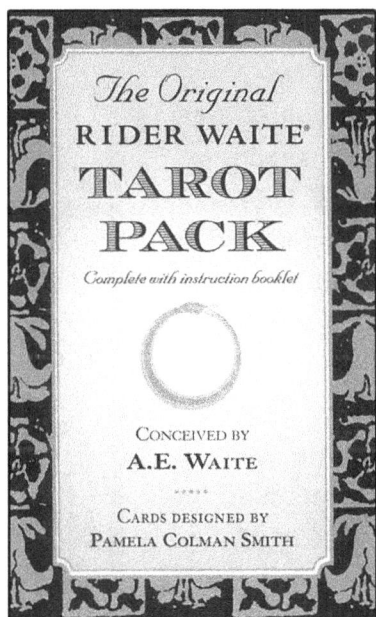

The Original
RIDER WAITE®
TAROT
PACK
Complete with instruction booklet

CONCEIVED BY
A.E. WAITE

CARDS DESIGNED BY
PAMELA COLMAN SMITH

BASED PRIMARILY ON THE RIDER-WAITE TAROT DECK

2013
a.d.

INTRODUCTION

The Tarot cards are familiar to most people and continue to sell well throughout the world. Often the cards are used as little more than a game, but many people truly believe that the cards perform a divinatory function of future and past events. We are toeing a neutral line in this book on the metaphysical aspects of the cards because, like so many other beliefs, it is up to the individual to determine what meaning, if any, the cards hold. In other words, the cards are what you believe them to be.

Court de Gebelin

The Tarot deck is divided into two Major parts. The Major Arcana, sometimes referred to as the Greater Arcana, consists of 22 pictorial and symbolic cards. The Minor Arcana, or Lesser Arcana, is composed of 56 cards, including Court and numerical cards. These cards are divided into four suits.

The cards of both Arcanas are used to express a concise image of symbolism that some believe offers a key to the mysteries of a secret tradition, whereas others find it as nothing more than an amusing game. Regardless of one's belief in the validity of the Tarot deck as a key to the occult, the cards hold a fascinating, albeit obscure, history and deserve their place of interest for many followers.

The exact beginnings of what we know as the Tarot cards are muddled not only in chronological history but in the birthplace as well. Although obscure in origin, variations of Tarot cards have existed in many societies of the past. The close association with standard playing cards is obvious but many experts trace a strong correlation between the game of chess and Tarot cards as well. Whether the Tarot developed from a unified version with both the Major Arcana and the Minor Arcana or from two divergent card sets is unknown.

An imprecision in tracing the roots of the Tarot cards is that many experts cannot agree on what symbolic and esoteric forerunners truly led to the present day Tarot deck. Furthermore, there is a great deal of discussion on the composition of the present day Tarot deck even in the proper sequence of the Major Arcana and, of course, the symbolic representation of the cards themselves.

In 1781, Court de Gebelin suggested that the origin of the Tarot Cards was Egyptian and the 22 cards of the Major Arcana correspond to the Egyptian book, "The Book of Thoth."

Gebelin Tarot Cards circa. 1781

Gebelin also cites that the name of Taro is an Egyptian word representing the royal road of life. He suggested that the Egyptian version was spread throughout Europe, first by wandering gypsies and then further by expansion of the Holy Roman Empire. Gebelin also gave an allegorical meaning to the four trump suits (the Minor Arcana). The sword or staff represented the sovereigns and the military leaders. The staves or wands represented the agricultural class. The cups represented the clergy of priesthood. The merchants and commerce traders were represented by the denier or coins.

Gebelin's theory of Egyptian origin was further espoused by Ettelilla (his actual name was Alliette and he reversed his name of publication) and it was he who captured the imagination of the cards as an insightful look into the soul by the practitioners. Eliphis Levi, a philosopher and an abbey of the Roman Church, initiated the idea that the cards were a sacred alphabet of Cain's oldest son, Enoch. The progression carried through the Egyptians and to the Greek tribe who later founded the city of Thebes.

The occultism of the Tarot was significantly furthered by Gerard Encasse who wrote under the name Papus. It was he who also associated the 22 cards of the Major Arcana to the 22 letters of the Hebrew alphabet.

It was Arthur Waite who developed the symbolism of the popular Tarot deck into a cohesive presentation of symbolic

Gerard Encausse (Papus)

ideas that appeal on an universal level. First published in 1910, it is Waite's Tarot deck that is familiar to most people. Most of the illustration utilized in this book come from Waite's book which was illustrated by Pamela Colman Smith.

THE MAJOR ARCANA

It is the Major Arcana that most people associate the Tarot deck with, so much so, that people who first begin to delve into the Tarot are often surprised that another 56 cards exist. Even though there are 1000's of different versions of the card sets, remarkably the overall symbolism of the cards is fairly consistent worldwide. One of the more debatable aspects of the Major Arcana is if they have reversed meanings or that the cards carry a positive and negative image regardless of what position they are laid out in.

The Major Arcana cards, sometimes referred to as the emblematic card, carry a strong symbolism and are often associated with a narrative story of life through the order in which they are numbered. They have a strong tie in with different philosophies of different civilizations and since they are present in so many, the determination of actual origin is difficult to narrow down. The next 44 pages show different artists' interpretations as well as some general attributes given to the cards.

2 0
1 3
a.d.

0

THE FOOL

THE FOOL

Illuminates a newly discovered talent or a dramatic new path in life. Can also indicate that a lack of foresight can cause problems in the future. Often personifies the spirit and enthusiasm of youth and rashness.

**O
ZERO
O**

THE FOOL

DIVINATORY ATTRIBUTES

Passion, folly, foolishness, infatuation, pleasure seeking, irrationality, mania, immaturity, ridiculous, indiscretion, carelessness, frenzy, extravagance, obsessive, thoughtless, inattentive, intoxication, delirium, shortsightedness.

REVERSE ATTRIBUTES

Indecision, negligence, hesitating, apathy, vanity

**Illustration on facing page by
CHRIS CALDWELL**

2 0
1 3
a.d.

Signifies the divine motion in Man and of the unity of the individual being on all planes. Life is a game of chance offering circumstances in which the only control realized, is based upon one's individual capabilities.

I
ONE
I

THE MAGICIAN

DIVINATORY ATTRIBUTES

Imagination, diplomacy, creativity, originality, self-reliant, spontaneity, self-confidence, willpower, self-control, trickery, self-determination, skill, dexterity, ingenuity, flexibility, influential

REVERSE ATTRIBUTES

Insecurity, delay, ineptitude, indecision, self-destructive, disgrace, disquiet.

Illustration on facing page by
JOHN MARROQUIN

2 0
1 3
a.d.

II

THE HIGH PRIESTESS

THE HIGH PRIESTESS

Indicates a teacher that is able to assimilate knowledge and pass it onto others. As well as dispensing knowledge, the Priestess also protects. She is the spiritual Mother and Bride and some consider this as the highest of all Major Arcana cards.

II
TWO
2

THE HIGH PRIESTESS

DIVINATORY ATTRIBUTES

Self-reliance, foresight, serenity, tenacity, learning, objectivity, mysterious, wisdom, practicality, emotionless, comprehensiveness, objectivity, understanding common sense, instructive, perceptive, platonic, impatient

REVERSE ATTRIBUTES

Ignorance, conceit, shallowness, selfishness, unsympathetic, surface attractiveness, shortsightedness

Illustration on facing page by
MARK BLOODWORTH

III

THE EMPRESS

THE EMPRESS

Symbolizes female productivity. Works in subtle ways as well as direct. The Empress is concerned with personal values and possessions. This card symbolizes materialism rather than spiritualism.

III
THREE
3

THE EMPRESS

DIVINATORY ATTRIBUTES

Level-headed, fertility, material wealth, accomplishment, development, action, attainment, marriage, children, female influenced, practical, decisive, intuitive, fruitfulness, motivational

REVERSE ATTRIBUTES

Infidelity, vacillation, anxiety, delay, loss of interest, distractions, inaction, self-doubting, wasteful

Illustration on facing page by
DONALD ENGLAND

IV

THE EMPEROR

IV

Indicates a person ready and able to assume responsibility. The situation or person is based on a sound intellectual basis of reason rather than emotional or intuitive ones. A self-awareness that one is on the right path.

THE EMPEROR

THE EMPEROR

DIVINATORY ATTRIBUTES

Stability, accomplishment, confidence, conviction, masculine, reasonability, husband, father, brother, leadership, strength, authorative, dominating, competence, firmness, wealth

REVERSE ATTRIBUTES

Ineffectiveness, benevolent, compassionate, feebleness, indecision, obstructiveness, immaturity, petty, weak

Illustration on facing page by
SETH DAMOOSE

2 0
1 3
a.d.

V

THE HIEROPHANT

THE HIEROPHANT

Usually indicative of a situation rather than a person, this card symbolizes traditional values and possibly religious influences. Attention must be paid to previous experiences, not only of the questioner but of others experiences as well.

V
FIVE
5

THE HIEROPHANT

DIVINATORY ATTRIBUTES

Marriage, alliance, rituals, ceremonies, humilities, merciful, servitude, forgiveness, inactivity, lack of conviction, conformity, religious, spiritual, stoic, heritage, inspiration

REVERSE ATTRIBUTES

Generous, susceptibility, society, vulnerability, weakness, impotence, frailty, over-kindness

Illustration on facing page by
VINCENT LOCKE

2 0
1 3
a.d.

VI

THE LOVERS

THE LOVERS

The obvious symbolism of love and romance are just one meaning of this card. It can also indicate friendship and even business associations that will influence the reader. Can also indicate that personal feelings will blind oneself to the true state.

VI
SIX
6

THE LOVERS

DIVINATORY ATTRIBUTES

Attraction, love, beauty, perfection, harmony, honor, confidence, trust, infatuation, optimism, speculating, yearning, tempting

REVERSE ATTRIBUTES

Unreliability, separation, frustration, untrustworthiness, fickleness, failure

**Illustration on facing page by
TED WOODS**

2 0
1 3
a.d.

THE CHARIOT

Usually when this card is presented, it tells of a hard labor or task that is forthcoming whether it is a specific project or task, there is likely to be a struggle. Attention must be paid to details.

VII
SEVEN
7

THE CHARIOT

DIVINATORY ATTRIBUTES

Escape, turmoil, triumph, vengeance, trouble, war success, perplexity, productive

REVERSE ATTRIBUTES

Quarrel, dispute, litigation, defeat, conquered, overwhelmed

**Illustration on facing page by
ROBERT KNIGHT**

VIII

STRENGTH

STRENGTH

Can be used to indicate that a sickness is about to pass or that a long outstanding obstacle is finally going to reach a final determination. Also serves as a warning that one must utilize strong self-determination and resist temptations.

VIII
EIGHT
8

STRENGTH

DIVINATORY ATTRIBUTES

Strength, courage, fortitude, confidence, tireless, action, fervor, determination, energy, conviction, accomplishment, heroism, virility, triumphant, liberation

REVERSE ATTRIBUTES

Weakness, despotism, discord, impotency, tyranny, indifference, abuse, petty, sickness

Illustration on facing page by
DEREK ROOK

2 0
1 3
a.d.

IX

THE HERMIT

THE HERMIT

The questioner should exercise caution and prudence, especially if an important matter is at hand. It is time to look inside oneself rather than rely on the advice and input of others.
Knowledge obtained can sometimes be a burden.

IX
NINE
9

THE HERMIT

DIVINATORY ATTRIBUTES

Discretion, vigilance, prudence, misguided, self-denial, withdrawn, circumspection, desertion, annulment, insincerity, treason, expressionless, corruption

REVERSE ATTRIBUTES

Rashness, premature, concealment, disguise, fear

Illustration on facing page by
BRUCE GERLACH

X

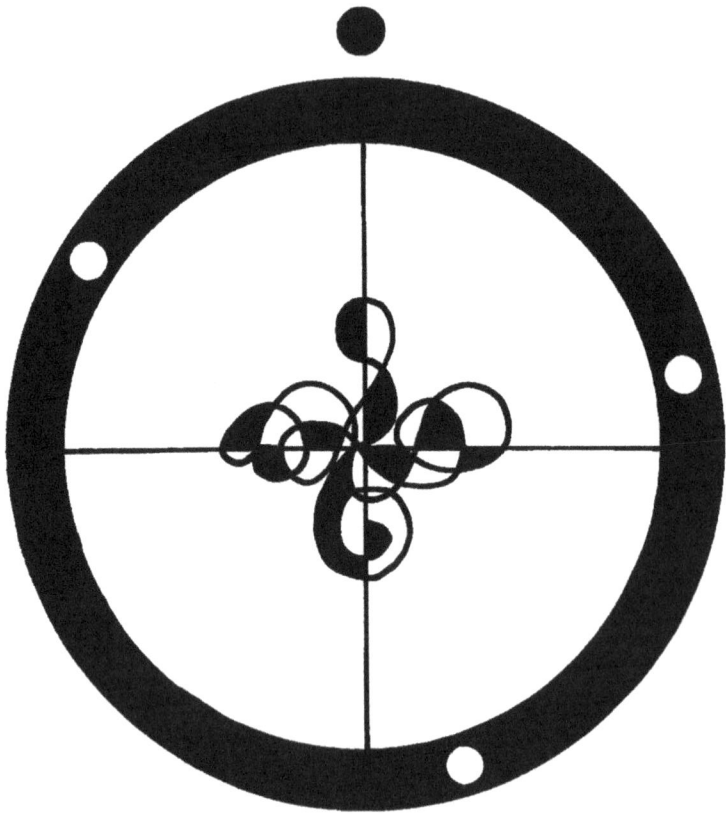

WHEEL OF FORTUNE

WHEEL of FORTUNE

Changes are in store. The changes can be positive of negative and they can occur due to direct action of the questioner or it may be just pure luck. Cautions one that everything can always have a plus and minus side.

X
TEN
IO

WHEEL OF FORTUNE

DIVINATORY ATTRIBUTES

Destiny, fate, fortune, success, luck, inevitability, progress, advancement, culmination

REVERSE ATTRIBUTES

Disrupted, failure, bad luck, ill-fated, unfortunate, handicapped

Illustration on facing page by
AIMEE ANDERSON

XI

JUSTICE

JUSTICE

Deals with fairness and justice but is not just restricted to legal matters. It can encompass any aspects of partnerships or relations as well. Things must be viewed without self-compassion and fairly or one's own goals.

XI
ELEVEN
II

JUSTICE

DIVINATORY ATTRIBUTES

Equity, rightness, fairness, balanced, impartiality, self-satisfaction, honor, virtue, virginity, equilibrium, consideration, executive, poise, triumphal

REVERSE ATTRIBUTES

Intolerance, bigotry, unfairness, bias, complications, abuse

Illustration on facing page by
TONY CASTEEL

XII

THE HANGED MAN

THE HANGED MAN

XII
TWELVE
I2

THE HANGED MAN

DIVINATORY ATTRIBUTES

Transition, change, reversal, repentance, sacrifice, boredom, abandonment, renunciation, readjustment, regeneration, improvement, rebirth, surrender

REVERSE ATTRIBUTES

Preoccupation, selfishness, unforgiving, sacrificial, falseness

Illustration on facing page by
JOSEPH COOPER

2 0
1 3
a.d.

XIII

DEATH

DEATH

Contrary to popular belief, this card does not indicate the upcoming death of the questioner or of any one close. It actually means a big change is about to occur, one that will sweep the questioner completely into an entirely new direction. Past events lose their influence.

DEATH

DIVINATORY ATTRIBUTES

Transformation, loss, end, destruction, failure, alteration, beginning anew, change

REVERSE ATTRIBUTES

Inertia, lethargy, sleep, immobility, stagnates, unchanging

Illustration on facing page by
BILL PULKOVSKI

2 0
1 3
a.d.

XIV

TEMPERANCE

TEMPERANCE

A bad period is about to end, the struggle will finally culminate. It doesn't mean the results are positive but that all that can be done has been done…a resolution. Also indicates that everything should be approached with moderation and/or self-restraint.

XIV
FOURTEEN
14

TEMPERANCE

DIVINATORY ATTRIBUTES

Moderation, patience, self-control, confidence, compatibility, frugality, harmony, accomadating, consolidation

REVERSE ATTRIBUTES

Disunion, impatience, sterility, frustrations, discord, hostility

Illustration on facing page by
ANNA GARAVAGLIA

2 0
1 3
a.d.

XV

THE DEVIL

THE DEVIL

This card represents to the questioner that it is time to take accord on one's own actions. Assume full responsibility and don't let your conscience be over-ruled by the easy way out. Can also show that unfortunate circumstances are about to occur.

XV
FIFTEEN
I5

THE DEVIL

DIVINATORY ATTRIBUTES

Dependence, subordination, bondage, subservience, downfall, temptation, self-destruction, unprincipled, unethical, violence

REVERSE ATTRIBUTES

Release, respite, divorce

Illustration on facing page by
JIM DEMICK

2 0
1 3
a.d.

THE TOWER

THE TOWER

Of all the Tarot cards, this is the one that usually signifies bad news consistently. Security and previous beliefs are about to be shattered. Beliefs of long standing will be broken and could indicate a breach of trust. The questioner will be thrust into new situations with no idea of the results.

THE TOWER

DIVINATORY ATTRIBUTES

Change, termination, distress, breakdown, ruin, divorce, misery, adversity, calamity, undoing, setback, loss

REVERSE ATTRIBUTES

Imprisoned, stagnant, trapped, tyranny

Illustration on facing page by
TONY MIELLO

2 0
1 3
a.d.

XVII

XVII

THE STAR

XVII
SEVENTEEN
I7

THE STAR

THE STAR

DIVINATORY ATTRIBUTES

Hope, faith, travel, artistic

REVERSE ATTRIBUTES

Arrogance, impotence, loss, theft, delay

Illustration on facing page by
ANJIE CONWAY

2 0
1 3
a.d.

XVIII

THE MOON

Represents an area of unclear direction. Motives and results are poorly defined. No clear answer lies ahead. A great deal will depend upon outside influences which the questioner has little, if any, control over.

XVIII
EIGHTEEN
18

THE MOON

THE
MOON

DIVINATORY ATTRIBUTES

Danger, darkness, terror, deception, occult forces, error

REVERSE ATTRIBUTES

Instability, silence, inconstancy

Illustration on facing page by
NATHAN PRIDE

2 0
1 3
a.d.

THE SUN

This card deals on a more personal level rather than one of enterprise and business. Joy and happiness are near and will effect the questioner regardless of how other matters are coming out. Even unbalanced news will have a feeling of contentment.

THE SUN

DIVINATORY ATTRIBUTES

Success, materialistic, contentment, confidence, happiness, celebration

REVERSE ATTRIBUTES

No appreciation, delay, modifications, sadness when referenced to children

Illustration on facing page by
MV ROMANOVA

2013 a.d.

XX

JUDGMENT

XX
TWENTY
20

JUDGMENT

DIVINATORY ATTRIBUTES

Renewal, outcome, reward, retirement

REVERSE ATTRIBUTES

Weakness, simplicity, sentence, decision, deliberation, loss, separation

Illustration on facing page by
JASON WESTLAKE

2 0
1 3
a.d.

XXI

THE WORLD

Shows stability and permanence and gives one a sense of accomplishment and pride. Indicates how others perceive your accomplishments and how those accomplishments will affect the upcoming goals.

XXI
TWENTY-ONE
21

THE WORLD

THE WORLD

DIVINATORY ATTRIBUTES

Recompense, emigration, flight, change, success, approval, hope

REVERSE ATTRIBUTES

Inertia, fixity, stagnation, permanence

Illustration on facing page by
KELLY O'HARA

2 0
1 3
a.d.

THE MINOR ARCANA

The Minor Arcana, also known as the Lesser Arcana, is composed of the four suits of Tarot cards. The four suits are Cups, Swords, Wands, and Pentacles. Each suit has four court cards and these are the King, Queen, Knight, and Page (sometimes called the Squire). The court cards are sometimes considered as the "bridge" between the Major and Minor Arcanas. The remaining cards in each suit are generally referred to as the pip card and often are about the same as regular playing cards. They are number one (Ace) through ten. Many of the older decks had each of the suit card illustrated as well but as general interest in the Tarot deck has increased, focus has shifted almost entirely to the Major Arcana and the use of the Minor Arcana has been de-emphasized greatly. Below is a chart showing the different names that the suits of the Minor Arcana may be called and the correspondence with a regular deck of playing cards. To utilize a regular deck of cards as the Minor Arcana, just use the suits as listed below and the Jack serves as the combination of the Knight and Page and can represent the young and immature of either sex.

SWORDS (Spades)
Epees (FR)
Leaves (GER)
Piques (FR)

WANDS (Clubs)
Staves
Acorns (GER)
Scepters (FR)
Batons (FR)

CUPS (Hearts)
Chalice (FR)
Coeurs (FR)
Coppes (ITAL)

PENTACLES (Diamonds)
Coins
Deniers
Carreaux (FR)
Hawk-Bells (GER)

The gypsies used the Minor cards in their future telling to deal with people and the Major Arcana to focus on events. The use of the Minor Arcana to represent people coming into the Questioner's life is not restricted to just the Gypsies. Here is a general outline of what the card represents when is utilized a card as a significator (chosen by the reader to represent the questioner):

KING — mature men, at least 35 years old

QUEEN — mature adult women

KNIGHT — young adult men

PAGE — children and young of both sexes

CUPS — blonde hair, light skinned

WANDS — brown hair, light skinned

SWORDS — dark hair, dark complexion

COINS — dark hair, very dark complexion

The following pages take a brief look at each of the four suit cards that comprise the Minor Arcana.

KING OF WANDS

Illustrated by Terry Pavlet

SWORDS

Swords are generally representative of courage, authority, boldness, force, ambition, strength, and aggression. The suit of warriors and leaders, the swords also indicate trouble and strife and sometimes are associated with travel having to do with water. This suit is the most ominous of the four.

KING: A man, probably dark, who is invested with power or authority, either moral, mentally, or worldly power of some kind. Has a strong influence via this power over your life. This is an experienced man of ideals who is the person that can handle any crisis that you may need handling. If reversed, the power will take on a malign aspect and will be directed against the inquirer and is sure to lead to unhappy consequences.

QUEEN: A dark woman who may have an evil nature and has an influence on the inquirer because of the respect an profession she has. Reversed, she is the type to spread or create scandal. This woman could also lead to loneliness and/or marital problems.

KNIGHT: A dark young man who can be an aid to you but is not to be trusted. Very assertive and a swift decision maker. In the reversed position, he is likely to disrupt your friendships and turn people against each other as sacrifices to his own ambitions.

PAGE: Usually indicates a rival in matters of love and someone who is perceptive in matters that don't appear apparent to the questioner. In the reverse, is someone who betrays your friendship.

QUEEN of SWORDS.

KNIGHT of SWORDS.

TEN: Unhappiness, sorrow, depression, financial woes. *Reverse- A slight but temporary gain.*

NINE: An attack on your credibility, someone is going to take advantage of you. *Reverse- Suspicions will be levied against you, relationships (more business than personal) will suffer.*

EIGHT: Quarrels, illness will occur. *Reverse- An accident, one that is associated with blood.*

SEVEN: A successful business action, a bright business future. *Reverse- You are dealing in a lost cause, especially if involved in a court case.*

SIX: An unexpected visitor or message. *Reverse- An unexpected gift comes your way.*

FIVE: A loss or deep sorrow to the questioner, an advantage goes to your enemy even though it may not be against your benefit. This card is same either way.

FOUR: A religious experience of influence. *Reverse- A disaster occurs.*

THREE: A commotion uproots a stable environment. *Reverse- A relationship is shattered, possibly a separation or divorce.*

TWO: A former enemy wishes to settle peace. *Reverse- Same, but the offer is not genuine.*

ACE: Your actions, though successful, will incur someone's wrath. *Reverse- Same, but you will smooth things over.*

PENTACLES

The suit of pentacles is generally considered for matters of money and property. The suit of merchants and traders, this card suit is associated with business, financial matters, and occupational goals.

KING: A person who is astute in business and could be very valuable to the questioner, however is generally unsympathetic to the questioner. Can be brought over if there is mutual benefit. In the reverse position, he will take a hard and unfriendly stance against the questioner and could cause trouble if the questioner continues to push.

QUEEN: A generous and charitable woman who would be a valuable ally. Honest, reliable, she is an expert in money negotiations. The reverse situation will reveal her toughness and materialistic attitude that make her a formidable enemy and if she and the questioner get into an antagonistic business argument, she will win.

KNIGHT: A previously unknown man who brings potential scandal into his dealings. A quarrel and bad feelings will occur between this man and the questioner if the reverse position of the card is laid down.

PAGE: A bearer of either sex, of good news in the upright position and in the reverse, is the same except the news will be bad.

KNIGHT of PENTACLES.

KING of PENTACLES.

TEN: A large gain of money.
Reverse- A small gain of money.

NINE: A steady source of income will be generated. *Reverse- Financial matters will be in constant upheaval.*

EIGHT: Financially, an even keeled and regulated income. *Reverse- Financial matters will be in constant upheaval.*

SEVEN: A gift of monetary value. *Reverse- A financial situation will occur that will cause hard times, may be short lived.*

SIX: Disputed matters in money, possibly a lawsuit. *Reverse- An unexpected resource will be made available to you.*

FIVE: A windfall will come your way which will compensate for a previous loss. *Reverse- A slight gain is yours but will cause legal obstacles.*

FOUR: Associations with the right people will pay off for the questioner. *Reverse- Social outreaches will cost money with no gain.*

THREE: Indicates a new business venture or project. *Reverse- The project will not be a complete failure but will have minimal results.*

TWO: Financial affairs seem to be a difficult moment. *Reverse- A surprise in monetary matters, but it is dependent on other cards to determine if good or bad.*

ACE: The beginnings of a new project that will pay off big. *Reverse- Same, but rewards will be small.*

CUPS

The suit of cups is associated with romance, marriage, and material goods. Often, they deal with relationships on both personal and business matters. Usually an indicator of the more humane aspects and deal with the beliefs that the questioner may have regarding specific people.

KING: Someone who genuinely cares for the questioner. May be a bit possessive but intent is good. In the reverse position, the intent is real, but failure to carry out goals and the unreliability causes a problem for the Questioner.

QUEEN: Has a great deal to offer and comfort the Questioner but sometimes is a little self indulgent. A mutual mistrust may develop between this person and the questioner mainly due to suspicion of each others motives in the reverse position.

KNIGHT: A very good friend and one that will respond as asked. If card is reversed then either through negligence or just unable, this person will let the questioner down.

PAGE: In this case, the page represents more of a situation than a specific person. Time to step back and reflect on where things are going. The reverse is the same, but questioner is likely to rush headlong into something that could be averted if a little more thought went into the matter.

QUEEN of CUPS.

PAGE of CUPS.

TEN: Stands for the general impression the questioner gives to others. *Reverse- Same, but someone who is close to questioner causes status problems.*

NINE: A very good card, a great event is about to happen. *Reverse- The great event will be slighted by an action of the questioner.*

EIGHT: An unexpected friendship or love relationship will develop. *Reverse- A period of intense happiness is coming.*

SEVEN: An unexpected turn of luck will cause good fortune. *Reverse- Same but not totally unexpected.*

SIX: This card influences other cards turned with it. If upright, then other cards refer to past. *Reverse- Other cards are yet to happen.*

FIVE: Beneficial in both love and money as matters come to a happy conclusion. *Reverse- Unexpected arrival of friend.*

FOUR: Love relationship is at a crucial juncture but still salvageable. *Reverse- A new and important friendship is formed.*

THREE: A long term project will pay off in a huge success, more than even imagined. *Reverse- An accident or disgraceful event is about to occur.*

TWO: A general indication of favorable love and money matters. *Reverse- A slight wavering in matters of love and money.*

ACE: Good news in plans. *Reverse- A change in plans but still a positive outlook.*

ACE ꝏ CUPS.

III

VII

WANDS

The suit of wands are usually associated with negotiations of some sort. These can be in legal matters, business, clubs or societies, or any other group associations. The card of laborers and workers, this suit usually represents modest and humble persons. This suit is also closely aligned with travel plans.

KING: A friend of the Questioner but not one to be relied on. He is usable for information and advice but not someone who the questioner should count on. If the position is reverse, then it is evident that he is full of empty promises and if the questioner relies on him, mishap will occur. This man will promise more next time but again he will fail.

QUEEN: Someone who truly desires to help the questioner and will do whatever she can. She is someone who makes sound judgments in both personal and business matters. If reverse, this person will get wrapped up in own affairs and neglect to carry out prior arrangements. Her reasons are justified but the results are the same.

KNIGHT: Will be helpful to the questioner and makes prudent decisions. Reverse position indicate outside influences on this person will make him unable to carry out his true intentions.

PAGE: Mainly associated with travel, this person will bring good news on you travels. But if the card is reversed, through this person's carelessness or extravagance, a minor disaster will occur.

QUEEN of WANDS.

KNIGHT of WANDS.

TEN: Travel likely to a new place. *Reverse — Take caution, otherwise the trip will go wrong.*

NINE: Good intentions and loyalties will lead to success. *Reverse — Disloyalty or cutting corners will come back to haunt you.*

EIGHT: A meeting with a person who will become influential. *Reverse — A dark haired woman will cause you trouble.*

SEVEN: An upturn in business affairs. *Reverse - Business will reach a crucial step and the wrong move could cause disaster.*

SIX: A project will be a complete failure. *Reverse — Indicates that a project that is failing is doomed so cut losses now.*

FIVE: A major decision will bring success to an undertaking. *Reverse — Tragedy in business or love.*

FOUR: Activities of enjoyment will lead to a financial benefit. *Reverse — A stumbling block to success will present itself.*

THREE: Wealth and fame are indicated. *Reverse — Plans made now will pan out in the far future.*

TWO: Unexpected trouble will cause problems. *Reverse — A message will be received and other cards will determine if bad or good.*

ACE: A major project is undertaken. *Reverse — Project will run into difficulties and only extreme patience and care will make it work.*

ETTEILLA'S GREAT FIGURE OF DESTINY

At right is one of the classic layouts for a divinatory reading that was devised by Etteilla. It utilizes most of the cards and is an elaborate but thorough reading system. The manner in laying out the cards is as follows. Take all 78 cards and shuffle completely. The Questioner cuts the deck three times with his left hand. The deck is placed face down and the Questioner will choose one card to represent himself. The card deck is then again shuffled thoroughly and again cut three times and put face down in a single stack. The deck is then laid out in the manner before in the sequence as number of Etteilla's figure.

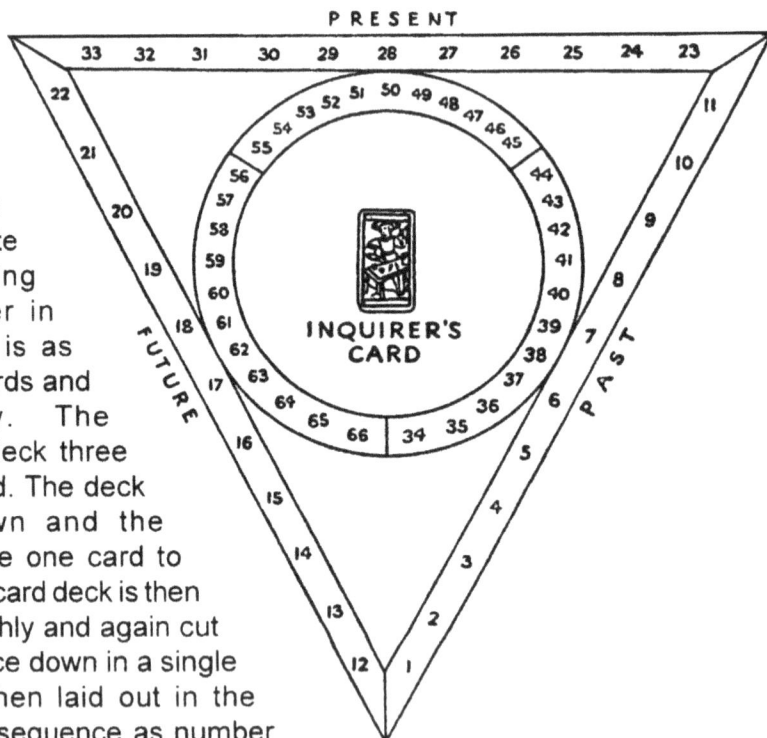

PRESENT

33 32 31 30 29 28 27 26 25 24 23

22 21 20 19 18 17 16 15 14 13 12

55 54 53 52 51 50 49 48 47 46 45

56 57 58 59 60 61 62 63 64 65 66 34 35 36 37 38 39 40 41 42 43 44

INQUIRER'S CARD

11 10 9 8 7 6 5 4 3 2 1

FUTURE

PAST

As can be seen by the chart, the present is indicated by the two upper rows. For each turning over of the cards, one card from each row should be turned. Both cards are then read together. Starting on the right side, Card #23 would be read with Card #45, then Card #24 with Card #46 and so on until the present rows are finished. The future is read last and starts with Card #12 and Card #66. This too is read upwards.

In all the many various forms of spreading the cards, the readings are only as good as the interpretations and relationships that are read into them. It is always important to stress the interdependence of the cards with each other. There are 1000's of divatory schemes devised and most readers have their favorites.

CARD SPREADING

The methods of spreading the cards to obtain the readings of those cards differ a great deal among people. There are no established guidelines for the Tarot cards and one expert may propose one way while totally disregarding another expert's method. Whatever way one wishes to lay out the card there are some general guidelines that should be followed. First, all cards should always be flipped over in exactly the same manner and this is usually in the side manner so that a card that is meant to be reversed or inverted is not inadvertently flipped opposite of the intended meaning. The cards should be in order prior to shuffling so that the questioner who shuffles the deck will be using his influences to change the order of the cards. When the cards are turned over, it's always viewed from the reader's (or interpreter's) position, not the questioner's. The reader is the one that turns the card over.

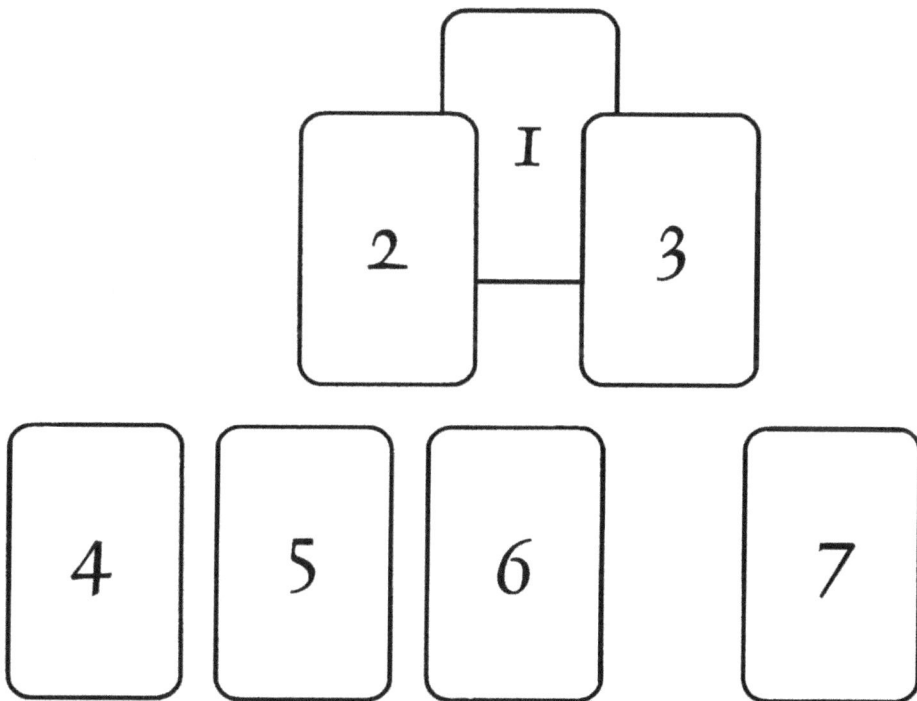

One of the easiest spreads is the Question and Answer spread shown above. It is mainly for a simple Yes or No answer. The cards are chosen as follows and laid out in the position diagrammed above. After the deck is shuffled, the questioner chooses one card that represents himself (the signafactor). The deck is reshuffled and then two more cards are laid down which will act as a guide to the problems with the situation or question. The deck is again reshuffled and then three cards are laid down and these will represent an answer to the question or problem. Again, the deck is shuffled and this final card will serve to illuminate the after effects of the question and/or solution.

TEN CARD
SPREAD

This is one of the earliest spreads known and one of the most common. Usually it only involves the twenty-two Major Arcana cards and the rest are set aside.

CARD 1: PRESENT POSITION
This card represents the Questioner and indicates what conditions are presently existing and the parameters which all the other cards will affect.

CARD 2: IMMEDIATE INFLUENCE
Represents current obstacles or influences affecting the present position.

CARD 3: DESTINY
This card clarifies the goal of the first card and the Questioner itself. What is to be accomplished?

CARD 4: DISTANT PAST
Illuminates previous influences on the current condition. The events signified by this card have already occurred.

CARD 5: RECENT PAST
Circumstances that have just recently occurred are occurring already that influence the present condition. Can also be used to indicate past events from some time ago that have re-manifested themselves.

CARD 6: FUTURE EVENTS
Upcoming influences that will affect the present condition.

CARD 7: THE QUESTIONER
Orientates the Questioner into the proper alignment. What is the true present position?

CARD 8: ENVIRONMENTAL FACTORS
Indicates the influence of the Questioner and actions thereof and how it will affect others.

CARD 9: INNER EMOTIONS
The innermost feelings of the Questioner, not what is being consciously projected, but the true anxieties and fears.

CARD 10: FINAL RESULT
The result and culmination brought about from all the influences of the other cards.

TEN CARD SPREAD DIAGRAM

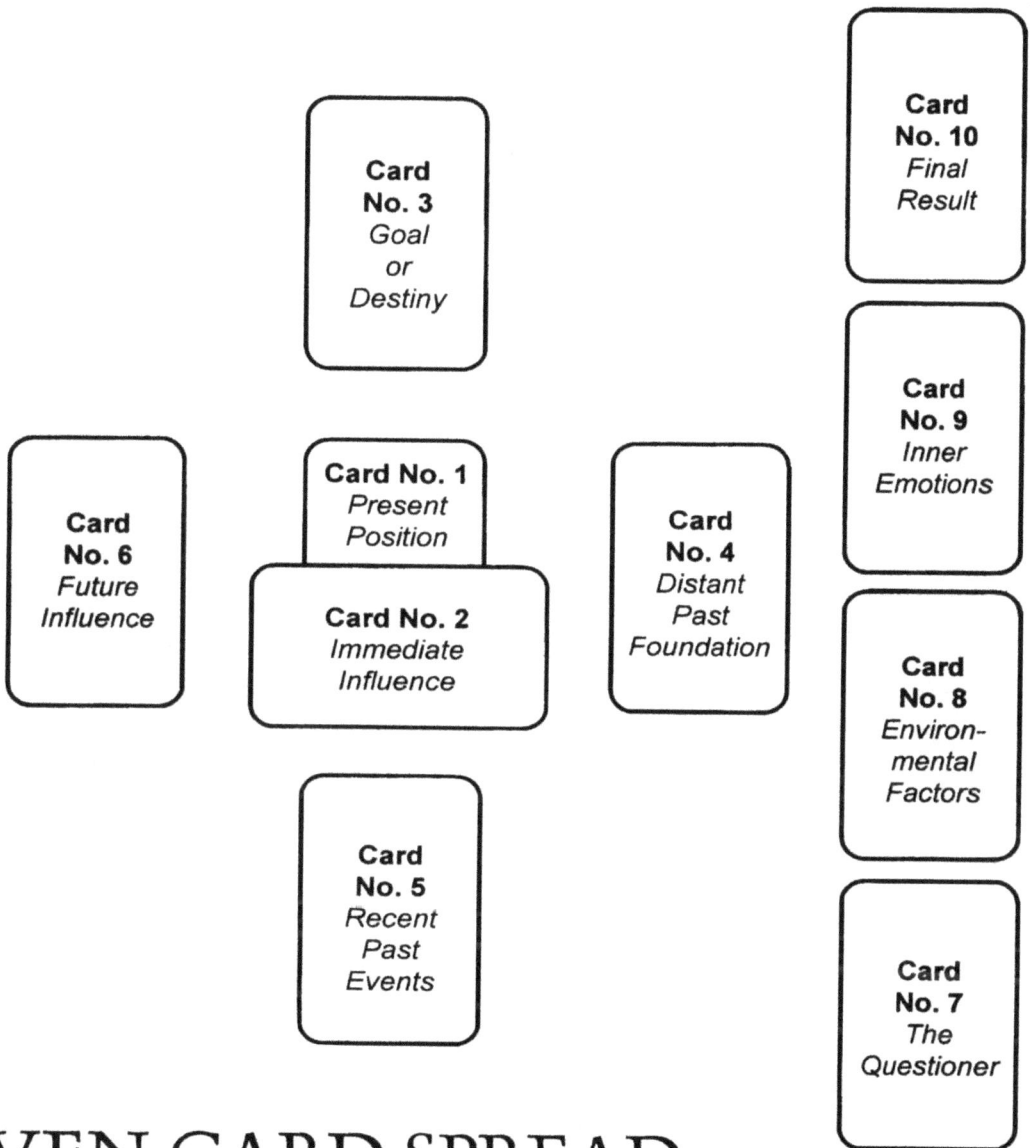

Card No. 3
*Goal
or
Destiny*

Card No. 10
*Final
Result*

Card No. 9
*Inner
Emotions*

Card No. 6
*Future
Influence*

Card No. 1
*Present
Position*

Card No. 2
*Immediate
Influence*

Card No. 4
*Distant
Past
Foundation*

Card No. 8
*Environ-
mental
Factors*

Card No. 5
*Recent
Past
Events*

Card No. 7
*The
Questioner*

SEVEN CARD SPREAD

This is a simple spread that utilizes a random selection of 11 of the Minor Arcana and all of the Major Arcana. It is primarily used for a direct "yes or no" answer. Usually, if four or more cards are inverted, then regardless of what the cards say, the answer is no.

CARD 1 - Distant Past
CARD 2 - Immediate Past
CARD 3 - Present Influences
CARD 4 - Present Obstacles
CARD 5 - Present Outlook
CARD 6 - Future Influences
CARD 7 - Ultimate Result

TAROT CARD ILLUSTRATORS

AIMEE ANDERSON – WHEEL OF FORTUNE
Aimee is a huge fan of Mother Nature, cats, and lemonade. She is a severe slacker when it comes to housework, paperwork, and any other kind of work. Aimee has no travel plans: "Other places are nice to visit, but Earth is home."

MARK BLOODWORTH – THE HIGH PRIESTESS
Artist of the award winning *Deadworld: The Last Siesta* (IDW) and also *Clive Barker's: Hellraiser*. He drew *The Ripper Legacy* and *Jack the Ripper*. Mark also wrote and drew *Midnight Mortuary* and *Nightstreets*. Recently, Mark has created original sketch card art for 5finity, Breygent, Versicolor and Galans Sketch Cards.

CHRIS CALDWELL – THE FOOL
Chis is a graduate of the Joe Kubert School of cartoon and graphic art, with over 15 years as an illustrator and designer. Projects include a nationally syndicated comic strip for the American Cultivator newspaper, *Cracked* magazine, and *Killer Diller*.

TONY CASTEEL - JUSTICE
Tony has been drawing since he was able to hold a pen which means some 34 years. He is influenced by erly pin up art styules of the 50's and 60's as well as the art of Oliva. His goal to inspire others to apprecieate fine art.

ANJIE CONWAY – THE STAR
Anjie is the founder of Artwerks Studio and focuses on a wide spectrum of art from digital to traditional – from pop to simple art for art's sake. Anjie's art has been used for fundraising charity events in recent years including the American Red Cross and Hurricane Sandy.

JOSEPH COOPER – THE HANGED MAN
Joe is known for his now infamous *Baby's First Deadpool Book* and also illustrated *Deadpool* and *Ka-Zar* for Marvel Comics. He has worked on *The Flash* for DC Comics and other projects for Image and Dynamite. Joe currently draws *Jim Butcher's Dresden Files: Ghoul Goblin* for Dynamite Entertainment.

SETH DAMOOSE – THE EMPEROR
Seth co-created *Xenoholics* and supplied designs and artwork for *I HATE Gallant Girl*, as well as the *Brat-Halla* webcomic and short stories to the *Nightmare World* series in addition to a short story in the *Masks & Mobsters* series. Currently Seth lives in Michigan with his beautiful wife and daughter.

JIM DEMICK – THE DEVIL
Jim specializes in black/gray pencil portraits. Jim's latest work was featured in Gary Reed's *Voices from the Deadworld*. Jim has also done freelance work for Sarah Jezebel Deva on her first solo album, *A Sign of Sublime* and has had his work featured in Jeff Belanger's book *Our Haunted Lives*.

DONALD ENGLAND – THE EMPRESS
Don's work can be seen in *Voices from the Deadworld*, covers for *Eerie Tales* and he's currently working on the comic, *Vaultwraith* for Razorback Records. Don has also worked on the comic *Lethal Lita* and *Tales from the Ravaged Lands*. Also did the cover for Gary Reed's *Night Pieces*.

ANNA GARAVAGLIA – TEMPERANCE
Anna is an illustrator of comic art, Art Deco and fantasy illustrations that are displayed and sold worldwide through online venues and cons since 2007. Her primary mediums used are watercolor, ink, gouache, and oil. She has been a Commissioned Oil Portrait Artist since 2004.

BRUCE GERLACH – THE HERMIT
Bruce has worked on licensed properties such as *Star Wars*, *Indiana Jones*, Marvel, DC, *Mars Attacks*, *Voltron* and *The Warlord of Mars* for clients Topps, Lucasfilm, Upper Deck, 5Finity and Breygent. Bruce is the creator of *Muck Man* and co-creator of the upcoming *Pipedreams and Stoopid Stuf*.

TAROT CARD ILLUSTRATORS

ROBERT KNIGHT – THE CHARIOT
Robert has entertained audiences with his stories throughout the U.S.A. and Europe with the U.S.O., historical reenactments, and renaissance festivals. Now, his favorite tales have been collected in print! *Tavern Tales from the Axe n' Ale* includes a special artists' gallery and short stories for all ages.

VINCE LOCKE – THE HIEROPHANT
Vince Locke has been drawing comics and illustrations for nearly 30 years. His projects vary greatly and include; *Deadworld, The Sandman, A History of Violence,* Cannibal Corpse CD covers, and work for the Cartoon Network. He continues to draw and paint in Michigan with his wife and three sons.

JOHN MARROQUIN – THE MAGICIAN
John "boy" Marroquin is the creator of *Mesheeka.* He has worked on such properties as *Night of the Living Dead, Avengers* and *Deadworld.* John Boy is also one half of El Arto Press, along with Christopher Sanchez, they have published two anthology books titled *El Mariachi.*

TONY MIELLO – THE TOWER
Tony is the creator of *GAPO the Clown* since 2004. He's done comics based on the TV shows *Who Wants To Be A Superhero* and *Wolfman Mac's Chiller Drive-In* and has provided art for major trading card companies. Currently doing *Noisy Neighbors,* a comic strip for Real Detroit Weekly.

KELLY O'HARA – THE WORLD
Kelly is a portrait painter who has sold works internationally and shown for over a decade through galleries and venues around the Detroit area including CPop, 323East, and The River's Edge. She is a manager and artist for the Rainy Day Art & Framing Co. in Grosse Pointe Woods.

TERRY PAVLET – KING OF WANDS
Terry was first published by TSR at age 14. Has created works for publications such as *Print Magazine, The Society of Illustrators Annual,* and *The Art of H. P. Lovecraft's Cthulhu Mythos* among others. Clientel have included Disney, Image comics, Wizard of the Coast, Miller Brewing, Ballentine Books, etc.

BILL PULKOVSKI - DEATH
Bill has worked on projects for *Star Wars,* Paramount Pictures and Marvel. He is currently working on a project entitled *Portraits of Poe,* an illustrated collection of Edgar Allan Poe's works in graphic novel format, fine art print and a premium trading card set.

MV ROMANOVA – THE SUN
She runs Flyting Graphics which is a small, freelance graphic design company out of the Midwest. Areas of focus include pre-press/print setup; vector art and design; mixed-media painting; and traditional work with charcoal or ink. "Flyting" refers to the Norse practice of constructing elaborate insults in the form of verse.

DEREK ROOK - STRENGTH
Derek is a self-taught and self-made artist, utilizing the punk rock, do-it-yourself approach to most of his creator-owned work. He's illustrated for such notable titles as *Zombie, Halloween,* and *Deadworld* and can still be found delivering vigilante justice with his newest comic book imprint Rough House.

JASON WESTLAKE – JUDGMENT
Jason has worked on book covers, comic books, trading card sets, and contributed artwork for many publications and properties including *Transformers, Night of the Living Dead, War of the Worlds,* and more.

TED WOODS – THE LOVERS
Ted is a comic artist based in Ypsilanti, Michigan. He's worked for companies like Cryptozoic, Shot in the Dark Comics, and Reasonably Priced Comics. He self-publishes his comic *The Book of Love,* and is highly addicted to Mountain Dew.

DEADWORLD™

THE COMPLETE STORIES

Finally! All the Deadworld issues available in these new collections of books bringing every single issue of the official Deadworld canon into print. Plus the short stories appearing in other publications.

Archives:
The original Deadworld.
Collecting the first two classic volumes from Arrow and Caliber.

DEADWORLD ARCHIVES:
Books #1 thru 6 (Volume 1)
Books #7 thru 9 (Volume 2)
Book #10 (Standalone stories)

Current:
The on-going tales.

DEADWORLD CURRENT:
Requiem for the World
Slaughterhouse
War of the Dead
Restoration

Collections:
Collections of tales.
Original and classic tales in special collections.

DEADWORLD SPECIALS:
Bits & Pieces
Chronicles
Voices from the Deadworld

Series & 1-Shots:
Self Contained Stories.
Orignial graphic novels and mini-series.

DEADWORLD SHOTS:
Dead-Killer
Frozen Over
Realm of the Dead
Tattoo
Last Siesta

For more information on Deadworld:
www.calibercomics.com

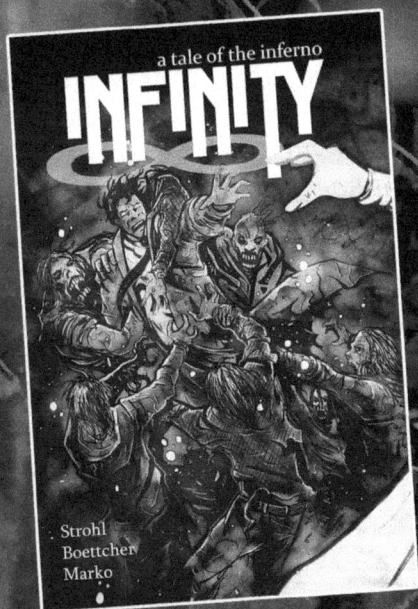

ALSO AVAILABLE FROM CALIBER COMICS

QUALITY GRAPHIC NOVELS TO ENTERTAIN

THE SEARCHERS: VOLUME 1
The Shape of Things to Come

Before *League of Extraordinary Gentlemen* there was *The Searchers*. At the dawn of the 20th Century the greatest literary adventurers from the minds of Wells, Doyle, Burroughs, and Haggard were created. All thought to be the work of pure fiction. However, a century later, the real-life descendents of those famous characters are recuited by the legendary Professor Challenger in order to save mankind's future. Series collected for the first time.

"Searchers is the comic book I have on the wall with a sign reading - 'Love books? Never read a comic? Try this one! ....money back guarantee..." - Dark Star Books.

WAR OF THE WORLDS: INFESTATION

Based on the H.G. Wells classic! The "Martian Invasion" has begun again and now mankind must fight for its very humanity. It happened slowly at first but by the third year, it seemed that the war was almost over... the war was almost lost.

"Writer Randy Zimmerman has a fine grasp of drama, and spins the various strands of the story into a coherent whole... imaginative and very gritty."
- war-of-the-worlds.co.uk

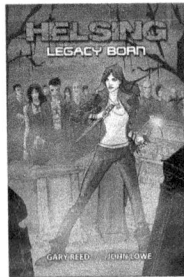

HELSING: LEGACY BORN

From writer Gary Reed (Deadworld) and artists John Lowe (Captain America), Bruce McCorkindale (Godzilla). She was born into a legacy she wanted no part of and pushed into a battle recessed deep in the shadows of the night. Samantha Helsing is torn between two worlds...two allegiances...two families. The legacy of the Van Helsing family and their crusade against the "night creatures" comes to modern day with the most unlikely of all warriors.

"Congratulations on this masterpiece..."
- Paul Dale Roberts, Compuserve Reviews

DEADWORLD

Before there was The Walking Dead there was Deadworld. Here is an introduction of the long running classic horror series, Deadworld, to a new audience! Considered by many to be the godfather of the original zombie comic with over 100 issues and graphic novels in print and over 1,000,000 copies sold, Deadworld ripped into the undead with intelligent zombies on a mission and a group of poor teens riding in a school bus desperately try to stay one step ahead of the sadistic, Harley-riding King Zombie. Death, mayhem, and a touch of supernatural evil made Deadworld a classic and now here's your chance to get into the story!

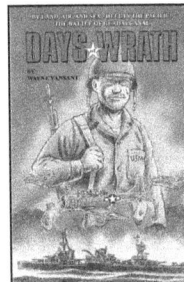

DAYS OF WRATH

Award winning comic writer & artist Wayne Vansant brings his gripping World War II saga of war in the Pacific to Guadalcanal and the Battle of Bloody Ridge. This is the powerful story of the long, vicious battle for Guadalcanal that occurred in 1942-43. When the U.S. Navy orders its outnumbered and out-gunned ships to run from the Japanese fleet, they abandon American troops on a bloody, battered island in the South Pacific.

"Heavy on authenticity, compellingly written and beautifully drawn."
- Comics Buyers Guide

THE BOBCAT

Described as the Native American *Black Panther*.
1898. Indian Territory. Will Firemaker is a Cherokee Black-smith who is finding out that the world of ancient lore and myth of his Tribe, that Will had always thought of as tribal fairytales, are actually true, and they're telling him he must replace his best friend from the animal kingdom, The Great Cat, as the guardian of his people. This sends him down a path of shock and disbelief as beings from the ancient past begin to manifest themselves in the world of reality. And as malevolent forces rise up in the wake of the fledgling Industrial Age, the future rushes head on into the Old West. Tahlequah will never be the same...

CALIBER PRESENTS

The original Caliber Presents anthology title was one of Caliber's inaugural releases and featured predominantly new creators, many of which went onto successful careers in the comics' industry. In this new version, Caliber Presents has expanded to graphic novel size and while still featuring new creators it also includes many established professional creators with new visions. Creators featured in this first issue include nominees and winners of some of the industry's major awards including the Eisner, Harvey, Xeric, Ghastly, Shel Dorf, Comic Monsters, and more.

LEGENDLORE

From Caliber Comics now comes the entire Realm and Legendlore saga as a set of volumes that collects the long running critically acclaimed series. In the vein of The Lord of The Rings and The Hobbit with elements of Game of Thrones and Dungeon and Dragons.

Four normal modern day teenagers are plunged into a world they thought only existed in novels and film. They are whisked away to a magical land where dragons roam the skies, orcs and hobgoblins terrorize travelers, where unicorns prance through the forest, and kingdoms wage war for dominance. It is a world where man is just one race, joining other races such as elves, trolls, dwarves, changelings, and the dreaded night creatures who steal the night.

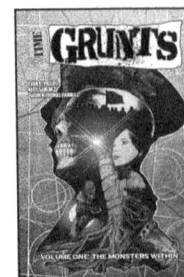

TIME GRUNTS

What if Hitler's last great Super Weapon was – Time itself! A WWII/time travel adventure that can best be described as *Band of Brothers* meets *Time Bandits*.

October, 1944. Nazi fortunes appear bleaker by the day. But in the bowels of the Wenceslas Mines, a terrible threat has emerged . . . The Nazis have discovered the ability to conquer time itself with the help of a new ominous device!

Now a rag tag group of American GIs must stop this threat to the past, present, and future . . . While dealing with their own past, prejudices, and fears in the process.

CALIBER
COMICS

www.calibercomics.com

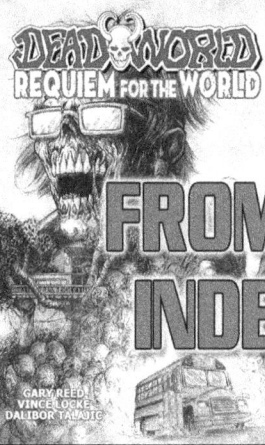

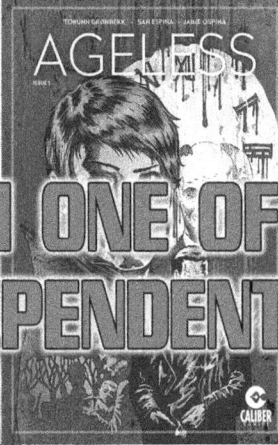

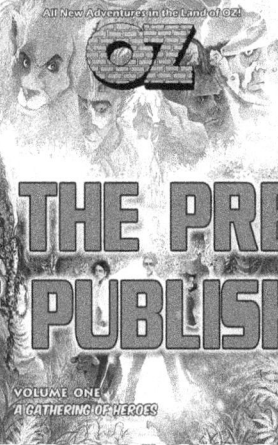

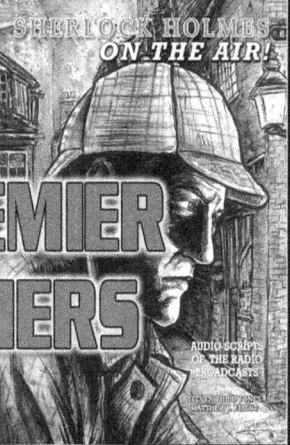

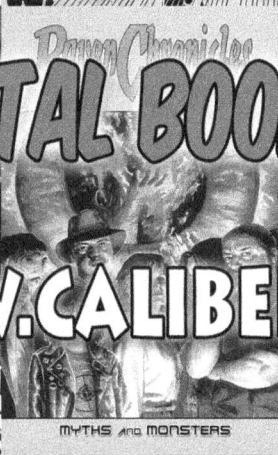